Dedication

I dedicate this book to my ancestors whom I've never met, to my grandparents, my parents, my brothers and sisters, to my daughter and grandson, friends, my children I never had, to my therapist, humanity, and the universe...and most of all to The Higher Power who gave you all to me. I appreciate you all for your wisdom knowledge and love that helped me to where

I 'am now in my life "off the couch".

"I'm off the couch bitch"

In the beginning I had peace and like the Garden of Eden to Adam and Eve it slowly drifted away from me. Stress creeped in causing her relative to attack me, his name was depression. The reason why I knew I had peace was after being married to the wrong Bigfoot for 19yrs, and moving on I no longer felt emotionally weighted down. I feel like a bird and I'm not flying, a horse trotting along practicing a kick. Damn I feel like a bowl of butter pecan ice-cream with a couple of fried plantains placed on top.

He was the wrong man for me he could very well be right for someone else it was a whirlwind of paranoid confusion. It all started in 1997 with a new job located in an at-risk low-income community, I truly loved my job working with low to moderate income families. I took a big cut in pay but my income didn't matter to me I adjusted; I was happy serving the community. It was like giving back my ten percent without having a toothache. I was always a naturally giving person it always made me feel better to give. To bless those less fortunate and feel blessed doing so, those of us who are like-minded we are the real chosen.

Giving in the sense of blessing a person with encouragement, a smile, going to stores outside of their community. A compliment, or even monetary if I had it to give. That was my way of giving back to The Higher Power for what was given to me. It was an awesome revolving door a blessing to be blessed to give blessings. No matter how minor or vast the giving... it will always be a blessing to someone in need. Imagine a world with that concept, yes, I know there will be freeloaders but how much can a poor person take if they are givers too.

One day while at work this tall dark drink came walking into the office. One of many tall and short dark drinks coming into the office with their perceptible swag. I would sit and laugh to myself because many of them act as if they were God's gift and that I should untie the ribbon and open the box. From my teens to middle twenties I had a relationship with my daughter's father. I dated a few guys and none of them worked out, it was always something stinking, drinking, drugs, or another woman.

At that time, I was and only knew about monogamous relationships. Within those years I was encaged opps!! I mean engaged and I couldn't go through it. Something, or call it intuition kept nagging at me saying "is that what you want for the rest of your life"? I kept thinking to myself "you know you have a loyal and committed personality… find someone who is worthy of your dedication and unbreakable love".

Most important a person who would reciprocate that same dedication and love you deserve. Being in tune with myself and what I will tolerate in a relationship kept me, and there was no kissing or hugging, no fantasizing, no nada celibacy was my last name. No smooth baritone high soprano silky music...a complete shutdown. A complete shutdown that only a dedicated priest, nun, or monk should have...so prayed up a wet-dream or should I say orgasm couldn't rear its lovely head.

At the time, I didn't know it was all a test, the biggest test of love, lack of encouragement, fear, emotional draining, and even the thought of murder. I was on the roller coaster ride of my life and the bar that goes across the seat that secures you in, broke... but I was still in the seat. Holding the bar close to me holding it tight praying I didn't let it go. The tall drink whispered all his punch lines "in one ear out the other". I'm laughing and singing lalalalalala "oh shut up" shoot I don't have time for that.

This tall dark drink was pertinacious, he kept trying to get me to drink from his cup. On his lunch break he would peak his mulish head in to say hello. He would ask me "if I had eaten" offering to buy me lunch, this joker! He was really persisted I ignored with a smile while saying thank you. I'm saying to myself "this dude" the hunt was on and it wasn't

America's most wanted it was a Broadway play called inevitable.

The test was in motion way before I got that job. The test was here before my tenth great grandparents. I went on and played the lion hunt with him and threw out little bits of meat in our conversations. I gave the lion some water to swallow that small piece of meat, and went out on a date. It was the thigh meat the dark meat that made me wrestle too.

Boom all those suppressed emotions of bottomless love and not having a fat wet sloppy jalopy kiss. What seemed like interminable celibacy was really five years of pent-up emotions that came out of me like a tornado on a rooftop. A hurricane with golf ball size hail, and six feet of snow. I was snowed in... couldn't move I didn't care if the fridge was bare or if the cat was feed (mu).

Fast forwarding to when I did come up for a burst of air after swimming in a whirlpool of emotional bliss. In 1999 the lioness allowed the lion to take her paw in marriage. It was beautiful at first having someone to take care of you, and you caring for him. Letting your guard down spending a little extra money. That tall dark drink was every woman's dream very attentive to my every need in the beginning, sounds like the bible. So thoughtful I learned not to mention aloud anything that I really didn't want, because he was there to make it happen.

The first to third year of my marriage was awesome, fourth to fifth year it needed two spark plugs and an oil change. During the fifth year it was horrible, a test for me, my marriage needed a new radiator, transmission, brakes and rotors. The coolant system needed fresh antifreeze not to mention windshield wiper solvent because I damn sure couldn't see the bird shit to come that was in my view. My marriage I thought was still solvable and okay comparing to the events that came from the neighbors of hell. Before I met my tall dark drink, I had what I thought was a beautiful older female neighbor who lived one door up from me that I shared recipes with.

At the time, I had long locks and she would dye my hair for me. We always set on the porch watching the neighborhood laughing and joking all the time, a real nice girlfriend to be around. But for the life of me I could never or I didn't want to see that when her other friends came over, she along with them gave me the silent treatment to where I was so uncomfortable, I made an excuse to leave.

As soon as I left, they would be over there laughing and giggling up a storm. If I came out the house onto my porch they would stop and start up again when I went in the house. Our houses were rowhouses and this was during the summer months and you could pretty much hear with your front screened door opened. So, I allow her to treat me like a hippo and the river was drying up-- and its nudging the crocodile to move over.

I thought maybe it was her company that didn't like me I get that from some women who are just mean-spirited with their low self-esteem. Her actions were definitely a form of control and I didn't like it especially when you're already nice and kind to people. On the other side of me was a male relative of hers who started dating this female from hell. One of many hundreds of women I saw climbing his fire escape leading up to his second-floor apartment. When he dumped her, she managed to rent the house next door between me and whom I thought was my older best friend. They both turned out to be a crocodile filled with diseases of pure wickedness.

Both started hanging out by that time I gave up trying to be her friend I was sick and tired of the petty gaslight games. However, they weren't finished with me the onslaught began with calling me names every chance they could. Coming home from work I would be called a bitch with evil looks, to me it was okay because it was no physical altercations. I was so happy they didn't touch me. I didn't have a problem doing the tangle with them if needed, it was the aftermath I was worried about. I didn't want to hear the words "book' em Danno".

They coaxed the neighborhood children to jump on top of my car denting the roof of my car. I rode around the city in a burgundy car with a huge dent about four inches from my head and when they saw that wasn't working. They would overturn flower pots on my deck out back throw trash in my yard and when that didn't bring a response. They sic the neighborhood drunk on me I had to run in the house. I didn't want to hit her and have it look like I took advantage of her drunkenness. Besides the blow probably would have killed her, I was trying my best to stay out of jail.

This huskbucket brought a dog and allowed it to urinate and defecate on her back porch. Hot summers would make it unbearable to enjoy my deck the miasma left behind in the air; it was unbearable. I started praying and doing a rain dance so it could rinse the stench away.

I caught this joker-huskbucket stalking me with her car one day she was riding very slowly behind me. Another day I was doing my yard work and set down on the lower steps of my deck to eat an orange. She and her then female roommate were eyeing me and when I wanted them to notice me observing them. They franticly jumped backwards into the house from their gang stalking. This woman was a bad vacation with no way to get back home. It's like being on a cruise and you didn't make it back on time from shopping, and watching the ship sail off into the horizon. Knowing you exhausted your credit card and you can't even call ghostbusters to help you. This woman would come out of her house around the same time my tall dark drink came home from work "to be noticed".

He never came home the same time but this huskbucket was right there stalking him too. In her tight seductive biker clothing or short skirts, and jeans trying to entice the tall dark drink. The reason why I knew this is because I would lookout for my tall drink to welcome him home. I was being that loving and caring wife to greet him at the door or meet him on the deck. That huskbucket wanted to greet him before I did, with her movie star enticing gesture when she said "heyyyyy neighbor". Well, he played the gaslight on me when I mentioned it to him. I stated to him "what a coincidence", and does he see what she is doing? His words "I don't see what you see".

So, you don't see nothing or noticed anything, not even every day for months of you pulling up from work. She comes out to go to her car and she conspicuously staring at you?

His response "Nope" I didn't know until later in the marriage that my tall dark drink loved that kind of warped distortion. He loved saying no when I said yes or vice versa, he would never confirm or admit to me other women's interest in him. I wasn't a jealous person it's just that he wouldn't validate the obvious because that was his way of conditioning me to doubt my intuitive nature or he wanted to take the bait.

After he said "Nope" I looked at him like hold up bubba when did you lose your sight and start reading braille. A good considerate tall dark drink would have said "yeah I see her but it's you I want, never mind her lets continue to ignore her". But when you are dealing with a self-centered egotistical personality and gaslighting is his last name they lack encouraging words to give comfort. Their encouraging words are used mainly for ammunition to advance information from others. Once they have achieved it, "believe you me" they have a galvanic comment in the barrel cocked and loaded to make you feel like a dummy for even dealing with them.

This huskbucket would coach her daughter to stand on her second-floor balcony and yell at my tall dark drink "what's your name, where are you going"? This little girl was a grown woman in a six-year-old body. Her voice was even husky as if she drank alcohol and smoked cigarettes in a bar lounge located near ocean city.

This gaslight gang stalking went on for maybe two and a half years by that time I started praying crying out to the Supreme Power of the universe to remove murder from my heart. Yes! the spirit of murder was creeping its ugly head their apparent actions and name calling along with my tall dark drink being absent of observation. His lack of compassion, consoling, reassurance, damn I needed some sympathy, empathy, or tickets to see a damn symphony from him.

It sure seemed as if peace was never coming my way again, I wanted another lesson in life. I was like the man of the book "take this cup from me" I can't take it anymore. I lived in a middle-class neighborhood that was trying to revive itself again. There were once doctors, lawyers, teachers a broad spectrum of professional people.

However, you know how it goes, jobs, the closing of black owned hospitals, fluctuation of drugs, liquor stores on every corner the intellectuals move out and the neighborhoods go down. In comes the neighborhood fast-food joints, bars and drug-dealers on every other corner. A cesspool of disease and corruption and being harassed constantly by malicious degenerate women. I see now why the spirit of murder was in the air I was breathing for what seemed eternal. To work in an at-risk community health center and sometimes dealing with folks void of manners. To come home and have absolutely no peace with the neighbors of hell. Plus, my marriage was failing the newlywed game by thirty points.

People generally acquire their malevolent frequencies from their upbringing, their lack of knowledge and training on how to treat your neighbors. The drug dealers respected me more, they didn't allow new comers to sit on my porch.

I gave them water in the hot summer months, introduced them to different fruits like kiwi, mangos, persimmons, and avocados they were only familiar with apples and oranges. I sliced juicy pineapples and shared it with them. It was really nice sharing with the young folks especially information from conscious African American books and cds. Schooling them on how they were contributing to the degradation of the neighborhood.

They said yes to the truth, but always came back with "we need the money".

They never disrespected me...even when they were running from the "popo" i.e. police and I would yell "run forrest run" when they came back around, I would be laughing and they would be too. They weren't good all the time it was shootings and death from that lifestyle. I know some of you are probably saying how come the drug dealers selling drugs did not bother you? The simple reason, they were children and I was teaching and giving as much wisdom, knowledge, and understanding. Sometimes they received it…and there was no malice or hatred towards me from them.

I would come home from the grocery store and some of them would stop everything to help me with my bags, they would often ask me "do I need help with the yard work"? And some called me mama. Okay, okay I hear you I'm getting back to the gaslighting huskbuckets and what she and her cohorts were doing… including my tall dark sour drink with his twisted gaslight ways. I tried taking this woman to court for harassment hoping it would slow her wickedness towards me.

It became extremely miserable coming home from work and not having any peace, the stalking, the looks, the name calling. By this time a new drug crew came in while the old crew was in jail and they started shooting damn near every day. I couldn't take it anymore I couldn't take my tall dark drink not supporting me when I complained of their wickedness.

While he's sitting there in the courtroom next to me not offering no testimony of that woman's behavior. Slumped in the chair with that look of "why am I here" sending that body language to the judge. I truly believe his negative frequency altered the decision in the huskbucket's favor. I was so stressed I cried and I ask The Most High to remove this murder from my heart. If she only knew how close I came to giving up my freedom; him included. That huskbucket didn't know what I was going through in my home with the phone calls from women calling in the wee mornings.

Waking me up the constant calls the harassment was off the chain (young folks' slang). With all that going on one day I sat up on side of the bed and it felt like I was sitting on a hard golf ball. I'm like what the hell is this some kind of intimate toy he brought in here? When I stood up the ball came with me to the bathroom and into the shower. First thing I thought was the big "C" word, and it's in my lymph node. It wasn't cancer it was an STD; I was so happy, that I didn't fuss much I just simply said "don't do that again". By this time, I was so apoplectic after every foul incident I've ever been through flashed before my eyes. I could taste blood and it wasn't because I just flossed or had gum disease.

I was in another realm a gray area no illumination, no sunshine in my eyes no rainbows not even raindrops to water my dim spirit. I was in a box with no holes to look out. It was like scraping my knee after falling off skates and no one there to treat it with peroxide and a bandage "no rubbing alcohol please".

As I drove to my older sister's house to borrow her ear because my dark tall drink was so sour. I couldn't deal with him coming home late not calling he was acting up at the time. I sat down to talk with my sister and as big sisters do at least my sister. She gave me words of encouragement she looked at me and said, "You have to look at people's intentions". Her statement to me scintillated like a Fourth of July, Chinese dragon firework festival all wrapped into one awakening.

My third eye was no longer blurry I could see now, it was ineffable and like a blink of an eye all that buildup pain and anger was gone. That song "I can see clearly now the rain is gone" depending on your age I can hear you singing the rest of the song. (wink)

Oh, how I thank The Supreme Master who orchestrated the release. It immediately came to me that the Almighty Power heard my cry and gave my sister the words to minister to me. As I'm writing this, I'll tell you later why I don't believe in coincidence. However; karma is like a monkey without a banana and a tree branch to swing on. All kinds of mishaps were happening to this woman, her daughter was taken from her.

One winter this huskbucket parked her car in the alley and it snowed. The snow was up to our hips and in some areas even higher. It was so much snow…it shut down everything. No one was moving that winter for some weeks. Please take a deep breath before reading the next sentence, I want you to read it in one breath.

Three weeks had past and this short skirt, thong wearing tight pants, motorcycle riding ding-dong of a woman. She couldn't get none of her associates to help dig her stank behinds out. The main streets were accessible cars were able to ride down my street, but she was back there by her mean-spirited self, digging for days. The thought of helping her had the nerve to cross my mind, all the crap she put me through. I heard something say "you better not" you better allow her to pass her test.

What I really wanted to do was yell at her and say, "God don't like ugly, ugly". I know you're wondering by now why this author is calling the women names...because I'm not a saint and at that time they were acting just like a huskbucket, wicked. However; if a saint went through what I went through; that saint would have murdered the huskbuckets in the tenth paragraph. After that she was evicted from the house, her clothes and furniture were set out on the sidewalk.

The older huskbucket who I thought was my friend and hers rumbled through the huskbucket's items. All the while laughing with her friends the ones that didn't like me. They laughed all day going through her stuff it was sad I wanted to laugh too. I wanted to gloat and say "nan-nanny nan-nan". However, my upbringing in apostolic holiness faith would not allow me to rejoice over people's sorrow, even if they deserved it "fighting good n evil". Plus, I didn't want karma or her brother to visit me again after easing up on me.

I later founded out the test of stress and depression was not finished with me. In the sixth year of my gaslight-marriage it went from an A to D, "D stands for dummy" it stood for downhill, disrepair, daunting, disrespected, dispiriting, decaying, disorder, disappointed, disingenuous, demoralizing. In 2006, we moved to a house he inherited although I had great reservation not to move with him, I went against my intuition. Thinking back with regards to allowing and putting up with emotional abuse, the abuse really could have ended in 2006.

By that time, I had gone through enough turmoil with my neighbors and him doing his dirt hiding behind working all the time. That damn job that he used to get his lovers, or friends to call him out to fix this or that. Not putting forth any effort to make time to strengthen our relationship as a married couple. Like that movie "Get Out" I missed the signs, clues, and the directions. Blinded by "he might change", love, and most of all by biblical loyalty. For years I waited for him to give me my walking papers, but it never happened.

The tall dark drink didn't have to, he had his cake and licked the plate clean. He had his stank huskbuckets he played with and me his house slave. Cleaning, cooking, yard work, ironing, washing clothes, scrubbing his white collars so he didn't look like a dirty dingy supervisor. All of that while fibromyalgia kicked my butt and the brain fog that came with it is freaking real, having colon cancer and colon resection surgery didn't help either.

He didn't put the work in to keep the train moving on the track, he only wanted to put the work in when the track was about to buckle and derail. That's when the tall dark sour drink would come in and fix the broken track and double checked to see if the switches were functioning properly "that brain again setting me up". When I saw his ability to get the train back on course that decision helped me to reconsidered moving to the other house. Another decision was the neighborhood started really deteriorating abandon boarded up houses were popping up like popcorn at the movies.

There were no strong neighborhood association the other drug dealers were sitting in the meetings intimidating the neighbors. The house that was inherited; it was a detached house. I was thinking if I move there and had a neighbor from hell it would be some distance between the houses. I wanted my marriage to last forever, "yes forever" that's why I married to him. I stepped over a lot of men... stepped over as in refusing their advancements, engagements, many of those men had deeper pockets than him "way more money".

I was marrying for true love not how much money he had I could have been married five to six times. I have the looks, the brains and the personality I chose him. I'm not that kind of gal to entice, seduce, or open myself up to a "single man" who I don't want.

Like I said earlier I'm not a jealous person because I know some people's strength can be weaken, but dammit at least fight it and try to be loyal and considerate. The only way to fight it, is with honest communication with a meaningful occasional date night. It's no difference than a church revival, a marriage has to be renewed. You have to put in the effort to cry out and praise your marriage...be steadfast. Don't renew it by bringing others into the fold, it will not work one or two will suffer in silence and eventually the balloon will burst.

So, I wanted to leave but I also took in consideration that he had just lost his mom and I couldn't leave him at that time. In the process of fixing the house before we moved in. The Higher Power gave me another sign that I should have stuck with that insight of leaving the marriage. Instead I thought I shouldn't leave him in his time of sorrow, and thinking of what other people would say. One day my sister's husband came over to detail my car the tall drink gave me and I got that burning desire to snoop or should I say investigate.

Seriously before I get to the snoop story…I really hate snooping when you must resort to that… deep inside you know it's related to distrust. I bucked up against snooping many times, I despised it I hated snooping, because I know most times it was the beginning to an end. So, I went on to snoop in my sister's husband's car and rode to the house where the tall dark sour drink was supposed to be working. I pulled up on him and two sisters one was on the porch and the other was standing close beside him.

I believe to this day she was one of many he was having affairs with. I got out of the car to speak and the girl haul tailed across the street. The tall dark stank drink turned and walked towards the house without even speaking to me.

Her sister on the porch in her patwah dialect said "she comma inna notha car oin yaw". That statement and them both fleeing in different directions right there told me everything I needed to know, but I didn't listen. Later on, Mr. Tall dark sour drink said, "He had nothing to do with that "fat ugly woman" he started fixing and, securing the track bed, laying down railroad ties.

Wiggling his way out of what I just witnessed, that fat hippy monkey ass huskbucket was after my tall dark sour-drink.

What she didn't know is I was already checking her out she always wore tight-wearing pants I noticed her when I use to visit his mom. However, that day she had on a long skirt standing close to my tall dark sour drink. That let me know she was checking me out because that was my attire long skirts and dresses "the old apostolic church". I don't know what the church is wearing now, probably thongs with spandex and skinny jeans. Believing him over what my brain just computed to me… and because he called her gross and ugly. I ignored the signs again deceiving myself that maybe with this move things would get better. But as my girlie girl, my daughter would say "whuttha hot-garbage" "the devil is a bald-head liar".

After the big move dating and enjoying each other came to a halt there was no communication nada-nada-nada. No regular touching, holding hands, love making, as they would say no "hit and miss" was the theme. Dinner time was lonely so I invited the T.V. and she taught me how to overeat and not pay attention to when I was satiated. Maybe because I was unsatisfied with my life and what was unfolding. Living with a stranger who no longer wanted to be my friend or was he in the beginning? I don't know! How can someone change like that loyalty, love, and consideration the definition stays the same so that person should stay the same, right? "Brain again".

My mind is spinning and I'm getting dizzy it doesn't feel like the dizziness you get as a child being swung around followed by laughter. This dizziness hurts it comes with headaches and thoughts of griminess.

Whenever I mentioned separation or even divorce, he would give attention for a short while, then back to the rotten normal. Thinking back that was gaslight being played on me over and over, and time again.

I delved into college with essays, projects, and clinicals all along suffering from excruciating sciatica pain that radiate down my leg throbbing. Suffering with neuropathy the top of my right toes felt like little Martians were pricking the top with sewing needles. I was suffering with restless leg syndrome the twitching was miserable. With all that twitching I should have lost weight in my thighs.

Fibromyalgia depression on top of depression along with that I had sarcoidosis that was in remission. I was still feeling the effects of widespread hard to the touch nodules that would sometimes be inflamed. One touch would send me to Jupiter where I saw a red sea with steam coming from it. In my self-motivated spiritual mindset, I repeatedly said to myself "you can do this". That damn fibromyalgia is like unto dominatrix except you don't need the big tall man or woman with a black skintight outfit waacking the hell out of you.

After two years in school I couldn't put back surgery off any longer I had two screws put in my lower back, lumbar area. After surgery, it seemed like what little self-esteem I had… was gone. I was so depressed I couldn't concentrate my mental agility said poof "see you later alligator after while crocodile". I allowed my being to be sucked into a tunnel of darkness staring into a black hole, nowhere to go. After back surgery in the hospital the nurses and my big sis were trying to get me up to walk. I smelled like what I believed a prostitute would smell like after having many johns without bathing. I'm like where in the hell did that odor come from, I haven't had sex in a year, had a hysterectomy I had no need to douche.

The thought that maybe the surgeon or hospital staff had their way with me while being sedated. The negative thoughts were running rampant but the question wouldn't go away "where did that smell come from" the smell from having semen in you for two hours or more after having sex. Don't act like you never had relations and rolled over went back to sleep till the next morning, and wake up stinking well maybe not the OCD people.

Well after back surgery I couldn't garden per doctor's orders, no bending at all…" holy hell". Still in the black hole unable to move I 'am afraid to move my foot one inch it might be the edge of the cliff. What has always allowed me to cope with life challenges, an acerbic marriage, and other people's opinions; was gardening. I didn't care about the physical pain that came afterwards.

My mind seemed rejuvenated serotonin was being released along with her cousins dopamine and oxytocin. The joy of a beautiful yard to look at was being threaten. Looking at a beautiful scenery was just as effective as doing the work. When I look back, I was my own psychologist and didn't know it" visual therapy ". Feeling all alone I couldn't get my floriculture-fix I needed to get my hands dirty. My feet needed to feel the earth as I dug up dandelions "dandelion wine" shushhhhh! Don't tell Eliot Ness.

I couldn't smell the scent of mulch or the fresh cut grass I miss the spiders, ants, and an occasional praying mantis.

The birds humming waiting to see what they could get from the digging. Most of all I truly miss meditation with gardening it's the best depression medication the Supreme Intellect made for me. I was definitely a lot smaller and agile but Ohhh! No! I couldn't help it I started gardening again; against doctor's orders. I could stay in the grass and weed forever cutting, weeding, and planting. Doctors should prescribe gardening before depression medicine I tell you it works if you can handle the physical aspects of it.

When I mastered meditating and weeding at the same time, sometimes I didn't feel no pain absolutely none " I was so in the now". But what I couldn't figure out is that after gardening about three to four hours later I couldn't walk; the pain was unbearable. This was each and every time after doing yard work it took a week for my body to cooperate "it was soooo freakin weird". Another incredulous ordeal was after the back surgery I couldn't watch T.V. The programs and shows that would project bodily trauma. I would get this abnormal feeling in my inguinal region. It was like an electric currency it's like I could feel the trauma being projected on T.V.

For an example I use to like watching skateboarding sports the kind they would jump onto a stairwell and glide. But when they fell at the same Planck time, I felt that bang, bump, clump, thump, clunk, clash, crash "okay you get the idea". What the hell was that, till this day no medical doctor has explain "why?" I'm thinking it could be some type of spinal frequency or something because it was also around the time.

I was experiencing restless leg syndrome and that sensation was horrifying also. Well I couldn't garden anymore that damn bitch ass depression hit me so hard. Emotional eating became an immense comfort and the worse nightmare in my life. I use to eat so much it backed up and they called it GERD gastric esophageal reflux disease and boy, not boi… that burned my throat, old folks called it heartburn.

I ate to suppress my feelings of sorrow…I needed to eat especially when I over ate it literally put me to sleep. I would eat high simple-carb foods like ice-cream with cake it really knocked me out like the song "mama said knock you out". I didn't want to deal with pain medicine tremendous fear set in. It seemed like drugs and alcohol addiction ravished both sides of my family and I didn't want that addiction. My food addiction was better so I thought I wasn't hurting anyone else "self-sabotage". My addiction didn't make me steal, lie, or cheat to get my fix, an unhealthy brain coping mechanism when it wants to hide from truth.

The truth is that some addictions can kill you faster than others however; all are reflections of one's self escaping a wretched reality. My addiction was slow suicide like my marriage in my confusion the food was putting me deeper in a situation, more into harm's way. I didn't need that extra weight 270lbs (XXL) on my frame after back surgery I was only 5'1. Whenever I came out of that high fructose coma only my cats were there to greet me, I thought they were the only ones that loved me. I believed that lie for a long time, for you see every now and then the neurons would spark again.

It came to me all that purring and rolling around was their seduction for cat food. Their bellies were "hanging too" from all that eating and laying around sleeping all day. My two cats had no fear of predators you could hear those jokers snoring loud, I would say to myself "isn't this some mess". They couldn't give a rat's ass about me. All they wanted was their cat food and a clean kitty litter. My mind was not working for me I was so confused on what to do.

All the while I didn't receive any emotional support from this tall dark bitter drink that came into my life and made me dehydrated. Yes! I can blame him for my some of my life situations he was supposed to be my rock when I needed foundation. He looked me dead in the eye and said he was serious about marriage too" in sickness and health, till death do us apart" I ignored the signs when we had serious conversations and I would remind him that I was his wife, he was my husband.

Which "he hated the title husband" I could see the microsecond reaction, but like everything else I played gaslight on myself too, lying to myself. I should have been a rebellious wife and not cook, clean, wash clothes, yard work and only focused on school work and got the hell out of there. Another gaslight moment years ago when I thought we were happy; he and I were invited to his co-worker's wedding. I went and brought a pretty pink dress heels, make-up "I was so cute".

We were walking around mingling and a woman that he knew a "co-worker, possible job wife" they started talking, nothing wrong with that but I was waiting for the introduction. "Oh so-n-so this is my beautiful wife" It never happened. Those jokers looked to be flirtatious the two of them could see eye to eye, she was tall also. The both of them steady talking looking into each other's eyes smiling at each other ignoring me. I couldn't believe it and I didn't want to make a scene didn't want to look like an unruly jackass… that stigma the reality shows portray black women today as.

I no longer wanted to look stupid so I scooted back to my seat like a wounded cat and waited for him to return. Sitting there embarrassed; smiling wondering who else saw what was happening, that shit was totally disrespectful. The next day I went shopping with my mom in Towson in the clothing store and "Lord and behold" it was the tall woman at the wedding party "I shouldn't call her huskbucket" but I will, that huskbucket had the nerve to look at me and speak.

I said to her "oh you're speaking now" she looks at me with a smirk that said "I had your man and can get him anytime". Looking back, I should have spoken with a smile and left it alone "show no chagrined". Because my response allowed that pig-huskbucket to wallow and think she had it going on.

When in actuality it's not problematic laying with a whore, especially if they stay cocked and loaded with the help of "soon come" stroke and heart erectile dysfunction drugs.

Meanwhile "back to yard work" I had to stop gardening so he had to do the yard work he had the nerve to get his short sneaky co-worker buddy. To help him with the yard work edging, trimming and cutting never once in my "too long of a marriage". He has never helped me with the yard work, I would have loved his company. I have invited him many times, but he never had time we could have used gardening to bond again. During all of this ordeal going on in "me" stank marriage life with infidelities, and surgeries I was in college taking prerequisites. I went and signed up for college on morphine using a walker that's how determined I was to complete what I started "sure did".

In school trying to get things back in order struggling emotionally. It seemed like I couldn't focus on school work. I would go into a trance the kind of tranquility you want when "only" practicing meditation. I didn't want to study with anyone I 'm like "what the hell is going on"? School wasn't never stressful to me. I thought the only stressor was my tall dark cloudy drink; and life at home or should I say "the house". I remember when I was having exams and clinicals back to back.

I noticed black discharge in my panties and it had the most horrid odor "oh Lord". It was so horrible I thought it was cancer or something. As fast as it came it left no smell, a clean natural smell and I was so into school. I did not see a GYN "I know y'all calling me names" but my very being...every strength I had left in me was towards school. Well two years went by no intimacy no nothing before then, it was hit and miss.

Today I see why it was hit or miss "keep reading and find out" during the absence of intimacy with my tall dark cloudy frog-like drink. My daughter was going through with her short brown jackass of a bitter-drink. An abusive drink that wouldn't hit another male drink his size. Ultimately, she had to come home, he sent her with just the clothes on her back. He took and sold everything to support his egocentric lifestyle. It was okay I knew she had the resilience to get back on track for "she was resilient" a fierce to be reckoned with, the spirit of TMH. She had in her what took me fifty years minus 10 to bounce back from a vague reality.

In college it was getting tensed there was an wicked-incident at clinical, a professor asked me to stay behind. She asked me to write a letter stating why I wear my hair wrapped. While she was asking me this her colleague who I just had clinical with was laughing damn near gasping for air. I said to her "it's for religious reasons" she said, "put it in writing."

I thought that was odd, but with all the terror in the world maybe it was law or something. "That brain of mine" making up stuff to protect myself from people. With that encounter of the third kind with the professors I left out and forgot to get my clinical sheet signed by the professor. The one who set there and laughed her heart out she should have pissed herself. I went to her office luckily the door was open, and said to her I forgot to have you sign this.

I apologized for interrupting her lunch but she said she wasn't going to sign it, I said "you have to". I was just in your class not ten minutes ago it's not like she didn't know who I was...she had a good deep in the belly laugh regarding me. She only signed it because I kept yelling please, please. She knew if not signed it's a no show and I will fail clinical she knew students couldn't miss one day of clinical... it was an automatic failure for that course. I was so stressed I thought constantly "why" why me why are these African American professors acting like this; why?

I said "this is some stank discrimination here" I worked with male and female Muslim doctors who covered. I saw Sikh doctors covered, Jewish men wearing Yakimas, turbans to traditional hats "get the crap out of here". The professor stated that many hospitals might have a problem with my covering. This prompt me to investigate so I called the hospital and spoke with the clinical coordinator and as I thought she said the opposite of what the professor said, and with that I will now call the professors "huskbucket".

I was so disappointed in those two huskbuckets who had tenure at an HBCU. A HBCU on North Ave in Baltimore, Maryland. I purposely went to when others were telling me to go to a University out of my community. They hurt my heart I could no longer trust them; they were trying to set me back with their sneaky ass discriminating hatred for me. "Damn professor huskbuckets". To make matters worse I sought out a lawyer and he said come in for a consultation, that joker took my money and the next day said he couldn't do anything for me.

I didn't have money to waste I wasn't working I was only focusing on school. He was a black prominent lawyer on Liberty Heights in Baltimore. I should have known better many of them have that boule mindset like those huskbucket professors. He probably didn't want to take on an

HBCU that he could have been associated with "thinking back, alumnus" I wanted my money back doggone it. Three hundred and some change to tell me no, I started thinking I'm in school for the wrong profession "son of a monkey". I wrote the letter to why I wrap my hair and along with that was my letter of resignation and it was nice I gave them history and I smacked that huskbucket upside the head with something to think about.

The letter was so sweet "professional" the head of the department along with my advisor had me in a meeting for two hours begging me to come back and stay at this college. I wanted a verbal apology and they should have had the professor in that meeting. I couldn't handle added stress from unprofessional sneaky conniving stank-ass professors. I was contemplating leaving due to the chronic pain and depression. I was still dealing with from surgery and its complications I couldn't handle the stress mentally or physically.

I noticed I couldn't spell or sound out simple words I knew I wrote them before, it's like I had developed dyslexia. To this day I'm wondering did I have it already and don't remember maybe "induced by stress" I always knew I had a teeny-weeny struggle in the confident department. I don't know if it came from watching T.V. as a child or seeing bumpy hair follicles on my legs "lol". With all this going on I decided to go to the GYN my daughter was going to, she was a nice older lady from India. One-month past I'm still in school thinking about changing my major to a profession not so stressful. Besides the HBCU administration said they would hold my resignation until I'm certain.

In my mind, I'm cheering I'm saying I've got to do this, get another degree something not as stressful. Negative thoughts of fighting to keep my license, what if I worked with sabotaging people. A career where there is no pulling or lifting since lifting and pulling is what caused my back issues. I can remember when I was caring for a lady who weighed at least five hundred pounds and she started to fall I caught her with my whole body. My knee was in her ass holding her up keeping her from falling on the hard floor.

My whole twenty-year-old life flashed in front of me like a speed of light. If this woman falls, I no longer will have a job, I will be evicted…my daughter will have no food to eat. I will have to move with people and start over. Bout time all that ran through this magnificent brain that finds time to torture me from time to time "negative fearful thoughts". It gave me the strength to lift that woman up onto the bed. Her wet shit was on my entire right leg seeping through touching my skin. Another incident I was working at a doctor's office and there was a file cabinet that had about six to eight thousand small and large charts.

This cabinet wasn't functioning properly, not more than one drawer was supposed to open. It should have had a locking system to prevent bodily harm, but all of the furniture in this office was used and beat-up. My desk had metal sticking out of it and one day it finally stuck me and caused bleeding and I needed stitches. However, that file cabinet's six drawers would slide out all at one time if you weren't careful. One day it did just that and the file cabinet started to fall on me, once again my life flashed in front of me. I don't know where that strength came from but I pushed that file cabinet upright off of me like an Indian elephant pushing a tree.

I didn't know it at the time but I was suffering from high functioning depression. From my teens to my now fifties there were definitely different levels of depression. My bouts of depression were like a roller-coaster; especially when this wicked dream. This nightmare of being naked hanging from my hands being whipped. I don't know where it came from but that dream haunted me from my early teens to my thirties. I'm wondering was its a past life regression? Maybe that dream was responsible for my lack of confidence. I've never told this not even to my various therapist "why did I feel shame"? I didn't want or asked for that dream but I 'am releasing it to the universe, it might help others to not be ashamed, afraid, or embarrassed. In the words of a dear beautiful pastor LYM who has ministered to me I release this because "you are not alone".

"Y'all keeping up" wink… so, it was a routine checkup at my primary doctor and he asked about my mammogram. Which sparked me to ask him did he get my pap smear from my GYN. Her office faxed over the result and it was positive for "trichomoniasis" he is looking at me I'm looking at him. He looks like he was more hurt then me I was numb because this brain just flashed. You mean to tell me I have been carrying this shit in me for two years or better. This tall dark tricky-dick frog of a damn monkey. That black grossly smelling crap in my underwear, that smell was worse than a decomposed body. Ohhhhh! My goodness not only that my brain said, and your black boule professors are treating you like white KKK supremist assholes, where's the difference.

I said doc is that an STD, he said "yes" I said "you sure" brain trying to protect again I have a headache! I explain to the doctor how I stayed in the bed for three days. Crying because of what the professors said to me and how they treated me. He wrote me a script for antibiotics and anxiety medication, till this day I don't know how I made it driving home. From the results of that Pap smear I cried so much my tear ducts dried up I went deeper into that dark tunnel. I was so damned depressed, and around the same time or somewhat later my second big sister was fighting colorectal cancer and succumbed to it. They say the colon cancer gene must run in the family. Years before my back surgery I had a colon resection due to cancer and my mom had the same surgery too.

That surgery left me with terrible IBS I have no oomph it drains my energy when the stool is trying to move through. Especially when I eat the wrong foods like breads, pasta, red meats, and potatoes heavy solid foods. I believe the area is where they cut and paste it back together "laughing at self". I even have to use gloves to retrieve it sometimes due to my sphincter it works when I can control my emotional eating. IBS is like giving birth you move forward, sideways, you squeeze, you push, your leaning backwards "laughing to keep from crying".

Like many other women and in my family hysterectomies are common. I had to endure that too another exorbitantly top depression badge added to my test. They say The Supreme Being doesn't put on you no more than what you can bare, but sheeeeeech. I'm still thankful to be here to give thanks and see the people I love. halleluYAH!!

I was so depressed living with chronic pain, the loss of my sister, not finishing college, living with an emotionless tall dark unholy drink. Let me just be forthright **"depression is a bitch"** and so is all its attributes. I know I went to apostolic church and there is a holy language and wicked language but I have every right to call depression what it is. It's worse than a four-legged dog, all dogs aren't mean and won't bite you. But this here depression is bad news there is absolutely no good in depression, none.

Depression can't be nice, it's no such thing as an elated depression. It will always be a mean, no good, conniving bitch. Instead of genesis stating to know "good and evil". It should have said to know "good and depression" that would have prompt Adam and Eve to google depression. Their asses would still be there and I would not have known depression so intimately. Depression is a spiritual disease that sucks the confidence of life from you and replaces it with fear and all of her or his characteristics.

No fight or flight to instantly help you get out of an acute stress, depression seems s-l-o-w. I thought of the word "slow" because of the word "low" in it, it definitely feels like it. That damn depression will have you up at night when you should be sleep, blowing zzzzz as the young folks say. It will take your will away from you, it will have you hollering to yourself "get up please get the f'k up now".

One of the attributes of depression is anxiety and I was trapped no education or job to render me freedom from this emotionless marriage. The universe was telling me that if I could just get out of this marriage that would eliminate some of the emotional stress. I had to make the journey walking my way back to health step by step with marriage being first, then deal with chronic pain. There are studies revealing some body aches and pains come from emotional stress overload.

But that brain of mine again trying to ease the pain telling me "your ancestors went through worse than this". To stay in the marriage keep trying better days have to come. I just wanted to be living by myself so I didn't have to feel or see what was contributing to sapping my soul. I could deal with chronic pain better than I could a no contact, loveless marriage.

It was like working with a co-worker who gets on your everlasting nerve. Talking about what they have and where they've been and that aura, I'm better than you. I'm saying to myself that, that co-worker is looking really good right about now at least I would get a break from them after work and on the weekends. I just didn't want to be like so many women and men who hold on for so long. That when the other party wakes up you are no longer in love, or like them. Plus, their ass is dried up form whoring and Cialis or vaginal cream no longer work for them "the devil is a bald head liar".

Well the gaslight continued It was times when I lost weight, he would ignore me like a centipede barrowing in the hot desert sand. As soon as I caved in and he saw me eating ice-cream, he knew my wall crumbled. In came the pizza, fried fish, Chinese food, and fast food whatever he conjured up, cookies etc. Many times, I brought the unhealthy foods too, but never once did he say encouraging words, no fingers through my hair saying "you don't need that food".

I developed this sickness of eating unhealthy foods to appease him so I could get a damn smile or a couple of words from this tall drink of crap. There were only three places I went to when I left the house the pharmacy, taking my grandson to and from school, or to the supermarket. If it wasn't for my grandson, may The Higher Power bless him forever I know for a fact The Higher Power ordered the steps, even though those steps removed him from his father's life. When I think back in time, I needed him. My grandson was the key that helped me see my reality and keep what sanity I had left; he was definitely an angel sent.

Let me list some more gaslight moments before I get to how I was able to "get out" as my islander friends would say "yes Lawd". You know how you see those small troubled waters, those signs but you ignore them to cope. I saw a glimpse when he always washed his car, he didn't wash my car next to his. That was weird but I tricked myself to thinking "oh he's tired" he does work harder than me. He would always call and ask did I want something from the store before he came home. I thought that was so sweet, but that was his way of staying out longer. He made it so complicated …he would call and say no mayo you like is at this store. Regardless of the item he used it to go to another store, even after I told him to get what was on the shelf "you better not think he really cared".

When buying time, he would offer to travel far to get whatever I wanted. Now I know some would say he was trying to please me; I use to think the same thing. But I know that tall dark slick-ass drink brought it on his lunch break and use that extra time to play the field. So, for years I always sent him on food missions or house items to make him happy.

He would get home and I would say we need this, he turned back around out the door like a kid in a candy jar "running after that trick". His gaslight tricks made me questioned my sanity I needed help, I started praying asking The Higher Power to guide me please.

So, I went to this neuropsychologist he did an EEG and the test showed good results, but "that brain" said to me. "I can't sit at no computer all day looking at beautiful sceneries" so I left there. Besides their billing department sucked, I would pay the damn co-pay I had to keep copying receipts to send to them. Something they already had I didn't need any more stress "whuttha hot garbage". Two years past and I started seeing a therapist actually I ran to the therapist she was on Fulton Ave in Baltimore she was awesome I'm very thankful for her contributions towards my mental health.

I know they are paid but I felt a sincere appetence about her to help others…that it was more than a job. I wish we could have been girlfriends because we would talk about some things about life that we laughed and if anyone really knows me, I love to laugh. So, she knew how to break that edge and encourage me to open up and talk.

Her office moved and I stopped going, discontentment and thoughts of me never healing from chronic pain still reared its ugly head. Depression medication making me hungrier brain foggier…a hot mess. I would leave therapy a beautiful atmosphere to go back to a stressful atmosphere that contributed to me visiting the sunken-dunkin place where they sell donuts "y'all still there".

My tall dark evil drink, yes evil cause what he did I will never forget, see how I said "forget". Because as far as I'm concerned, it's up to The Higher Power to forgive him not me. I'm thinking why should I forgive jokers and huskbuckets I didn't ask them to put me through life's test. I would rather forgive if it could help me forget what I've been through. It's nothing to forgive its done; all of life's test was either to strengthen me or send me straight to the coocoo koko puff farm. Sometimes I feel like I'm at the front door of the farm praying a horse doesn't open it saying he's Mr. Ed.

Let me tell you what this tall dark dung-beetle drink did, he would have me stalked, yep that really hurt me so. My driveway was right off of a busy street in Baltimore, MD so waiting to pull out was always an issue many cars were speeding like crazy. Most of them were police, ambulance and public servants trying to get to work on time. I lived down the street of a high school they turned into a training center for EMS workers, they were always speeding, slowing down enough to turn into the parking lot.

Every morning I would get up and take my grandson to school and I started noticing this black car parked across the street. Sometimes it was a woman or a man…I would drive out of the driveway and take my grandson as

I'm waiting for cars to pass by, that car would drive off. That car would be there across the street before we got in the car every morning "a hot-mess" this happened for months nonstop. I thought nothing of it at first because maybe they pulled over for a reason, maybe to answer their cell phone, who knows.

Like always I ignored it for a long time until I started noticing cars parked across the street in the afternoon. After I come from picking my grandson up from school and like the black car they would pull off as I parked in my driveway. I'm thinking maybe they're watching the house because we were robbed before, all along I'm mentioning this to that tall dark stank drink.

His words would be "that's a public street" steam coming from my head again even as I'm writing this. I'm like what person would not be concern that the house is being watched. So, I started watching the front and the back…why did I do that. Remember the fat hippy huskbucket remember she ran across the street to her house when I pulled up in my sister's husband's car.

Well she lived one door down from us, it always seemed that every time my tall dark stank drink was off, she was off and they didn't work on the same job. When he left her car left too, when he or she came home it was shortly thereafter the other came home. Instead of worrying about her getting trick I was concerned about these cars and trucks pulling up across the street and taking off as soon as I leave my car going towards the house. My grandson didn't notice it but I had to inform him in a way it didn't frighten him, so I said oh there's that black car again, must be our new neighbor.

The next time I would say I wonder why they drive off when we leave. He started noticing the black car leaving and coming and many times my grandson would play basketball on the driveway around 8:30-8:50 am before school. He would come in and get his bookbag or jacket and things and we would be on our way. This told me the black car came between 8:50-8:55 am we left out 8:55-58 am his school was only two minutes away. In the afternoons I noticed a white Mercedes, a red work truck...this green car a big gray truck had its share of stalking too.

One time my car was giving me trouble so I took it to the auto supply store parking lot at Wabash shopping center. Where many auto mechanics hang out waiting to service customers.

So, I had this mechanic man checked my oil and transmission on my car and he started bashing my brand name car. The name brand he liked was the brand my tall dark anti-freeze drink did not like, so the conversation became a laughing goofy conversation. I left there and went home I had a habit of sitting in the car when I pulled up to the backyard driveway.

Most times I would be talking on the phone with my daughter, mom, sister, or reading social media. While talking I texted my tall dark slick drink and said a mechanic said "your brand of cars is not as good as his brand". Do you know not five minutes later a big grey truck drove pass the front of my house, went across six lanes, three on each side and came up on the same side where the black car would park. I'm in my car looking the whole time at this joker pulling up across the street. He turned and look straight towards me the same truck. It confirmed many of my inclinations that the tall dark clown drink was stalking me. When I look back, he wanted dirt for our future divorce, damn frog. ***

I did some homework and saw that his manager-supervisor another possible job wife had a white Mercedes it also parked across the street. I showed the tall dark stank drink the video I took of her car and he erased it. Yes, I gave him my phone he had it in his hand looking at it and the frog erased it. I asked him why he erased the video he walked away like it was nothing. I purposely did that, him erasing it was a sign for me to keep my mind "wink". Well my grandson was doing his thang again playing hoops in the backyard and that black car pulled up across the street.

He came in the house yelling "grandma that car out there again". His excitement scared the hell out of me, my heart was pounding, and it literally felt like jumping out of my chest. I said okay "did they get out the car"? And he said "no", I had to do breathing exercises to calm myself down-- all the while telling myself "you can't keep living like this". After showing the tall stank drink the video... I started setting things in motion I needed to know affirmatively I was serious about divorcing him. One evening while the tall stank drank was eating dinner late as usual my grandson and I was watching a t.v. program. I mentioned the black car...so my grandson said "yeah granddad this car spying on us".

I mentioned that I was going to get my binoculars and get the license plate number and look the person up. Lawd and behold the black car started parking way up the street, remember when I said I don't believe in coincidence, not after living with that tall sour drink. My grandson said "granddad knows that black car" out of the mouth of babes even he knew that the black car had to be tipped off. The black joker in the black car started parking back in the same spot across the street so I could notice him again.

One evening my grandson wasn't feeling well with his allergies and cold symptoms coming on and he wanted to go to school the next day. I got up like 7:30 am the next morning and went to the nearest pharmacy. To get some over the counter medicines to "nip that cold in the bud" only old folks know that saying. I drove in the tall dark frog drink's brand-new car and not my low, slow, back hurting car. An idea came to me when I pulled onto my driveway so I backed in to face the street, I called my grandson. I told him that when he came out do not go to my car jump in granddad's car, and come out running. The black car arrived across the street like clockwork to torment me. My grandson came out running jumped in the car I zoomed to the end of the driveway. I was able to speed out and make that quick U-turn I caught up with the driver of the black car, it was the male. I pulled up and yelled at him and said "why are you stalking my house who are you" he looked at me like he was jumbled. He looked like he needed to be in a jungle with his monkey looking self.

I yelled I'm tired of you stalking me you bald headed monkey you, he had the nerve to say "I'm not bald headed" and drove off. My grandson said "grandma how you know" before he could finish the question I drove alongside the black car. The man lifted his cap and scratched his bald head, my grandson yelled "grandma he does have a bald head". How did you know grandma? He started laughing at the excitement we never saw his black ass or car again. In my car I keep a nice small compact binocular in my car for bird watching and one day I wanted to see who this black car joker was. I saw him without his cap one morning-- he didn't know I was in my car waiting for him like cat on a bird; sure did.

The evening stalking continued and when I looked back at the uncomfortable ordeal. I truly believe that tall dark stank drank stalked me through his associates to make sure I didn't bump into him and his dirt. He must have given them incentives him and his manager had that psychotic power to do so by sending co-workers and friends.

It's really scary when jokers are stalking you and you don't know why, don't know if there will be harm directed towards you. It's a horrifying feeling I already had a healthy paranoia personality, any escalation; "his stalking" gave me PTSD. Yes! This tall dark wicked evil acting drink and his cohorts didn't give a rat's ass about my mental health and the effects of stalking.

I don't care if one of his side-women were trying to get back at him by stalking me it's still his fault, he caused it. Maybe the tall dark cheating drink's lover wanted to lure me to a place. Where harm would be waiting or to see him cheating to prompt me to leave him. I sought another therapist an older man he was seventy years old, whom I love dearly for helping me see the insight. By that time my intuitive nature had taken a beating I was working with no frequency. I went to him and I was very transparent regarding my marriage he asked the right questions. I told the truth he asked "did we go on dates"? "I said no", what about vacations "nope" again.

I told him that my tall dark stank drank went on vacations without me, it made the therapist scratch his head. That must be a man thing when they lie or caught in something, or surprised they scratch their head. I expounded on how that stank drank went on two-week vacations and I didn't hear from him until it was time to pick him up from the airport.

Tall dark stank drank would call only twice when he got there and call to pick him up from airport. I took a lot of crap because of my health situations and he knew it was nothing I could do. People would ask why I didn't go with him, even if he tried to sweet talk me into going I wouldn't. I'm like this, if you can't take me out in the State, we live in how in the hell I look like going to that little island? My healthy paranoia kicked in, "you go walking along and accidently slip off a cliff" nah!! As the u-tube lady would say "ain't got time for that".

Some women would go with their spouses thinking "oh he loves me" and fall for the trap, not me. One time that tall dark stank drank went on vacation and when I went to pick him up from BWI it was him and this tall woman standing close. No one else was there, like a hundred feet away in all directions. It was the same closeness that I have with my computer typing this book damn near neck to neck, cheek to cheek. I really don't know if they were together, but if that was me and the opposite sex came up and stood with me.

I would have moved just because I wouldn't want my spouse to think otherwise, "consideration". I know I showed him and made him comfortable not being a jealous woman but damn you still couldn't think of me. If it was the other way around and he walked up to her and stood that close. He did it because he loved practicing emotional schadenfreude on me, he knew I was on my way. Before he started going on vacation by himself for years, I tried to get him to come home for lunch, he didn't have to stay on the job for lunch; to bond again.

I could work from home and he worked only ten minutes away one year. He would never come home I would cook salmon cakes, a salad no show the signs were there, but he never wanted a divorce. "I hear you saying I can't cook" "laughing" I can burn he never complained and he lapped it up like a hyena taking a lion's scrap.

I told my psychologist how we went from calling to texting to nothing, no contact at all. I mean all day no word, no "how are you doing today you feel okay"? I use to call him to see how he was doing even though there was no intimacy. I still cared and loved that tall dark stank drank, he was still part of humanity "Ommmm" But he would always say "I'm in a meeting" I got so tired of that statement we even fussed a little. He convinced me to text and damn if tall dark stank drank didn't text back "I'm in a meeting" we argued about that so eventually I got the message.

When he left out 7:30 am I didn't hear from him until he walked in the door 7:30-8pm. I didn't want him to go to the store for me I left him alone physically for years and it was time for me to emotionally detach from him. I was a good wife he never did without clean work clothes, food on the table, behinds in the air when I could trust him, I even cut his fingernails and toenails. Shit I know most women aren't doing that today or fifteen years ago with the feminist movement "I was making money too" I didn't mind, it made him feel good I felt good...everything was good.

I didn't care if I had a professional high paying career and he was a trashman if he came home and wanted his toenails cut. I would have soaked his feet and cut them I would not have sent him to the nail salon just because of a high income "that's how I am". I could do a better job anyway "smiling". My psychologist asked me an important question "can you continue to live within that situation"? Whoa!! I said to myself it hit me hard I saw stars even though that question was already dancing around in my subconscious. It was the way he said "think about it" his head was tilted a little to the side with such sadness and he said "the next visit we will talk about it".

He gave me some books to read that really opened my eyes "mindful awareness" books. I know most folks they want to rely only on the bible and their faith, but dang-blasted thank The Higher Power for therapist. That's what they're here for to pick away at the layers of people's opinion and evil deeds, and also to help keep you out of jail. I saw my therapist every Friday and when I went back, I kept the subject off the tall dark stank drank and home life. The fear is real not working so confused I didn't know my head from my tail, I was like my cats chasing my tail trying to find my head. My psychologist played along for a while and allowed me to elude talking about that question he asked me. Hey readers wake-up do y'all remember the question? "Laughing".

Three weeks past and during that time I asked The Higher Power for guidance I cried out I prayed my butt off. I asked The Higher Power should I leave him give me a sign pleasssse. I'm going back and forth because the bible said divorce was no good avoid it if you can. I asked the tall dark stank drink would he like to go to family counselling, he said "I don't need counsel". Still trying to save marriage well soon after that ingenuous prayer I started seeing numbers, yes!! Lawd. Numbers like 11 and 44, 1:11, 7:11, 2:44...it kept going on and on it was driving me crazy. I saw it on vehicles. I saw it on grocery store receipts my food prices were $311 dollars, $50.11 it was weird. I could be in another room that didn't have a clock and when I went to a room with a clock. To see the time or look at my cell, more times than enough. I would see 4:44, 6:44, 10:44, and 11:11 and so forth I started thinking maybe I have some type of build in magical timing frequency. But when I go in the bathroom then to another room, go in the room that has a clock and see 7:44, or 7:11 that theory went out the window.

There was no clock in my living room and I would send my grandson to see the time on the stove, and damn if he wouldn't come back 9:11 or 6:11 am or pm. I'm out shopping get in my car turn it on put seatbelt on look up at the car clock and dammit it would be something 11. It got so bad seeing numbers dealing with 11 and 44 I started putting fabric over my clocks in the house. I told myself this is ridiculous after a week went by, and when I remove the fabric damn if it wasn't 10:11 am "can you freak'n believe it". I told the therapist about the numbers and all he did was smile nod his head like he already knew my answer. After nodding he asked what is your plan for leaving, now I'm scratching my head asking myself "how he knew I made my mind up to leave"?

Unfortunately, my psychologist retired before I was finished driving him to smoke and drink but. Weeks later he called me and ask how I was doing and wished me well. I thank The Higher Power for allowing the time spent with such a beautiful soul. He was able to break through this thick wall of fear I'm so thankful. What's in the word fear (ear) guard your subconscious the gateway to peace in the mind and your piece of heaven on earth.

The universe is not finished with me yet, it sent me another beautiful humble intelligent soul, whom I will call by the initials M.S. Having this therapist in my life immediately after my psychologist retired, was truly a blessing from The Higher Power. I needed another brilliant therapist because I was making a pivotal move in my life that was so freaking scary.

For you see I gave up my independence I grew to living with someone allowing him to make the majority of the decisions concerning the household, and us. Most times I went along to get along; I wanted to be the good wife. Neglecting that voice from my grandfather who spoke to my subconscious forty-eight years ago.

He would say, and you have to say it in your country voice "Saunnndra don't let no man fart over you, ya hearrr me". They say knowledge is powerful, but words are keys to freedom years up the road. Waiting for you to fly to new heights hovering over new beginnings, zooming with delight.

My new therapist was and will always be dear to me. It seemed like every time I was feeling down, I would get a notification of a mindfulness video that spoke to what I was dealing with at that time. The proliferation of self-awareness books and or tapes shared... a spiritual connection indeed that I will cherish the rest of my life. The mellifluous voice and the facultative opinions that gave me insight which guided me to a greater awareness "I feel so blessed".

I started packing two boxes a day starting in February 2018. Thank The Most High Power for my grandson he helped me tremendously, some days I only had the strength to point my finger. Not one time did that tall dark sour drink help me pack, he went to work and came home. It was no honey don't leave me can we work it out, his mind was made up like mine was…no moving money either nada. If I have to use condoms in my marriage

I might as well be single, that's how I feel about it, besides I can't get with it if I don't feel loved I'm not that kind of gal. I guess he had so many people tugging at him he didn't need my attention anymore. Matter of fact he always wanted attention and I submitted, that's in my universal sign but damn I would like some attention once in a while.

All my belongings were packed and not to be bragging on my loyal, dedicated, loving, considerate, sincere self. Before I left my 18-year marriage in 2018 I transferred all utilities that were in my name to his name. I could have been very nasty and vindictive and had the gas and electric cut off, phone, t.v., internet, and house alarm too was in my name.

I could have let him worry about it when he got home, I made up passwords and gave it to him, so he could change it later. I could have had him paying for my car insurance even long after I acquired some. My raggedy ass car could have been double insured and waste his money, but I'm not that kind of gal. I never nagged about getting my hair or nails done, that stereotypical bull-crap that surrounds black women.

Never went out buying designer clothes or purses costing him big money, I could care less about someone else's name. Damn sure not going to buy it if the price isn't decent, I don't care how it looks. I love the simple life even when I get a million dollars for my books "law of attraction", wink-wink.

I will not spend it on other people who have made their names expensive, I would rather help those who need a nudge, a helping hand. Well I'm back home on the block I had so much turmoil with those huskbuckets I talked about earlier.

Yep, back in my row-house I brought in 1990s y'all know I cried but I didn't for long because that brain said "at least you have a home to go back too". In many parts of the world especially third world countries with comparison I lived in a mansion, that brain again. "Laughing". The day I left that tall dark selfish drink was on a day of symbolism we were married on the 12th and I left on the 12th 2018 same month.

Here it is 2019 haven't had intimacy yet, it's been eleven years damn there's that 11 again. It's been a long time since I've seen a beautiful healthy disease-free upright pyramid. I stayed true to the end loyalty is my middle name I knew I was divorced in The Higher Power's Eyes, but wanted to be in man's eyes. If I meet a man and he start having some insecurities he will never throw up in my face "I met you, while you were still married". I was talking with the pastor who ministered to me earlier and I mention to her "who's going to want me?" that woman of The Higher Power lit into me like a tornado lifting a house of its foundation and threw the bathtub a mile away.

She hollered at me and said "you have a lot to give" y'all know my brain said "yeah fat" stop laughing, who that is choking. She ministered to me "you are loyal, smart, honest, and your gorgeous, you still have a lot to offer a good man". Her words did help me look at myself differently, however, my subconscious wouldn't allow me to believe and accept me as I am.

What I could see was an aging, obese grossly overweight, many people told me I was beautiful, beautiful skin "but dammit they didn't see me naked". Oh, my goodness I didn't know over the years I tortured my body overeating to numb myself from life situations. Family woes or being in that marriage to encounters with wicked jokers. I will accept some of the turmoil of internalizing their wicked evil intensions towards me. I didn't know it was possible to block their negative frequency, I know now. The aftermath emotional eating is so devastating my body has lightning bolts from head to toe. If I bend over with my backside facing the mirror and look back. It's a horrific sight to see, that is not of god. Who in the hell has money for a great-grandma whole body makeover when your grandson doesn't have a child yet? There's fat pockets and flaps that permanent apron on my body "Whuttt tha hot garbage".

The fat under my skin looks like cottage cheese, feet wrinkle, and hands are wrinkle. I could see my hands being wrinkle because I did gardening without gloves. After cutting grass I would take my shoes off to feel the earth under my feet when I was planting and weeding. But hell, what does the top and sides of my feet have to do with it that brain said "at least you have feet". Even my calves are not as firm as they use to be mild muscle atrophy a hot mess it's like Jell-O where did my youth go?

I was "just" thirty-five years old twenty-three years ago and my legs, breast, and behinds were tight what in the world "laughing and crying at the same time". For the men who are reading and laughing at my comical descriptions you need to know that your ass deflates too. You lose elasticity in your skin, arm, and chest muscles they too show loss of definition. Some of you to have breast that could fill an A cup, your knees and feet look old too.

However, you turn your nose up to women your age with the same body changes. You know those young women don't love or like your sagging ass, you know damn well it's the money. With that being said you have caused older women to do what you have been doing for centuries, she now has to run after younger men spending money to listen to the same lies.

Anyhooo! Despite my war-torn body that I was carrying around, I started losing weight I had a dose of peace once I had settled in. I no longer craved fried, fat, greasy, cheesy, cancerous foods. Losing weight, what a boost to my self-esteem that was buried for years behind heartache, health issues, and emotional neglect. So, my message is no one is worth suicide by eating, and as my pastor would say "the devil is a bald head liar".

I no longer had to see that tall dark frog drink come home and immediately go back outside on the back porch. So, he could text and talk to whomever he pleased. Divorce was inevitable that marriage was feeling more and more like slow-suicide and as islanders would say "divorce soon come". It was a time he was getting a call from his supposedly cousin from Canada and she would call every Wednesday. Well one day he was taking a shower and left his phone downstairs and it rang, I answered it and the woman, and I mean if y'all could have heard that woman. She went on and on stating "I'm his cousin" she said that about six times, I told her "okay its fine" no problem.

It didn't make a difference to me saying it to myself so I stated to her "he's in the shower I'll let him know you called". I told him "your cousin from Canada called, call her back". Do y'all know that huskbucket stopped calling him every Wednesday? I asked him how come your cousin doesn't call anymore. He said "you answered my phone" I said "hold-up bubba" but, that's your cousin he eventually went to see her. Let me tell you of another cousin, she was a cousin-in-law in Florida we use to visit during the early years of the marriage. The doctor I use to work for let us use his half a mil condo so we would go and visit his blood male cousin, but the wife was suspect.

She has all the qualities of a sneaky somebody, and I don't mean dignitary we couldn't never click. You know how you can sense a phony ass person; I mean phony. She was pregnant and had the baby and we went to visit and this cousin had no modesty, unless she was in front of her husband. She would breast feed her baby with both breasts hanging out, point-blank topless in front of my tall dark goofy drink. I thought it was an islander thing with some of the women. But when I saw this huskbucket cover each and every time in the evening when her husband came home from work.

I knew she was a green bumpy female frog. The next man I meet will have only male cousins so I don't have to be bothered with kissing cousins. Hold-up! I forgot about those male cousins they can meet at that old town road and ride like they can't no more. "I got the gerbil up my ass dildo in the bag" I couldn't help it, it's just a lyrical joke. I couldn't help it, I'm still in therapy "lol" y'all still here.

Anyway; it was such a blessing to feel peace hovering over me again, it was a joy not seeing his unhappy face. Feeling that negative aura chipping away at my soul eating me alive. I was feeling that peace you would get from laying on the ground face-up surrounded by twenty acres of land with a beautiful house on the hill with a veggie garden out back. I was getting there I deserve peace... I deserve to be loved, and allowed to give love. To give it wantonly without reservation and know the recipient is loving, kind, and deserving. Yes!! Lawd. One more thing to tell y'all I was finished writing this small 6"x9" book after the Yess!! Lawd. But the number of words in the left-hand corner said 11711 if you add them up it equals 11, shut the front, back, and check the basement door while you're at it. I might as well keep writing to say if you think you're going through test in life, "you're not alone" keep fighting it… sit and listen to the Higher Power of the universe.

There are days I can't get out of the bed not being able to work, being afraid to work because I don't want to get fired, because I just could not get up. No matter how much I was cursing and yelling at myself to get the hell up. I even have job searches emailing me just to scan through the many jobs, longing wanting to work. It's like when I went on a ninety-one day fast all I kept looking at was mukbang videos yearning and watching people eat. I went back to eating the same ole same ole steaks, fried chicken, high carb foods, ice cream I know what it is, emotional eating divorce procedures started.

It cost me more to get a divorce than it did to get married damn shame that tall dark joker drink doesn't want to help a gal out. Even in my daydreams I longed for emotional serenity I stepped out with faith asking him to cover me as I make this next journey in search of peace and joy. I left a financially secured home when it dawned on me that if I stayed it would be a severe emotional demise. I'm like if I 'am going to feel alone I might as well be alone, step on in faith.

The tall dark stank drink was making six figures and when I left my income allowed me to apply for food stamps, yepppp below poverty folks by USA standards. No wonder immigrants flee here I didn't give a damn I wanted out and a taste of peace. Its miserable living with a person who no longer cares for you.

Sickness and health will prove to you if a person loves you to life or not. However; I nipped that spirit in the bud I went on another fast for fourteen days. To cleanse myself really good I'm currently a vegan now, trying it again. So far so good I haven't had to use the glove in a month... I want to know if it will help with inflammation, depression, back pain all of it. Living with fibromyalgia and sciatica is liken to a twenty-year bid in a Chinese prison however I'm looking for a parole hearing.

I'm praying veganism will be that gift to being independent again, eating healthy and taking aquatic exercise, some yoga, light massages. I want to ride my bike again I want to go back to college, work, go on a cruise, and go horseback riding. To an amusement park, roll around and make love on the beach like in the movies I know y'all laughing I'm serious about that beach get-together. To everyone who's going through trials and tribulations don't let it consume you save some willpower in your hard drive.

In your cloud, or one-drive so whenever you come across an unhealthy situation in your life you will have the strength to flee. Stay spiritually connected to the Higher Power read your holy books. As well as self-awareness books, listen to mindfulness tapes and or videos. Last but definitely not least seek a licensed therapist. Seek one that will help you out of the sunken place fortunately for me everyone I sought after contributed tremendously to me making significant steps in my journey towards wellness.

Even though I'm off the couch and out of that house I shared with the tall Bigfoot drink, unfortunately many of the illnesses that kept me on the couch follows me everywhere I go. However, I feel at peace I'll continue to work on self. The key to dealing with chronic pain, is to stay uplifted as possible and laugh at it. Maybe I can come back with book two and tell you about how I rode my bike for the first time in seventeen years, and that beach date went 'lol".

Inspirational Scriptures

Here is the list of scriptures that supported me spiritually and emotionally during my test…

Deuteronomy 31:8 And the LORD, he *it is* that doth go before thee; he will be with thee, he will not fail thee, neither forsake thee: fear not, neither be dismayed.

Jos 1:9 Have not I commanded thee? Be strong and of a good courage; be not afraid, neither be thou dismayed: for the LORD thy God is with thee whithersoever thou goest.

Psalm 119:48 My hands also will I lift up unto thy commandments, which I have loved; and I will meditate in thy statutes.

Psalm 119:76 Let, I pray thee, thy merciful kindness be for my comfort, according to thy word unto thy servant.

Jeremiah 17:14 Heal me, O LORD, and I shall be healed; save me, and I shall be saved: for thou *art* my praise.

Isaiah 41:10 Fear thou not; for I *am*

with thee: be not dismayed; for I *am* thy God: I will strengthen thee; yea, I will help thee; yea, I will uphold thee with the right hand of my righteousness.

And seek help through patience and prayer, and indeed it is difficult except for humbly submissive **Quran 2:45**

Is there any reward for other than good? **Quran 55:60**

And We will surely test you with something of fear and hunger and loss of wealth and lives and fruits, but give good tiding to patient

Quran 2:155

"O you who believe! Enter absolutely into peace Do not follow in the footsteps of satan. He is an outright enemy to you **Quran 2:208**

Your Lord has not taken leave of you, nor has he detested you. And the hereafter is better for you than the first. And the Lord is going to give you, and you will be satisfied **Quran 93:3-5**

"God does not forbid you from being good to those who have not fought you in the religion or driven you from your homes, or from being just towards them. God loves those who are just" **Surat al-Mumtahana, 8**

"The brightness of the sun, which lights up the world, the brightness of the moon and of fire - these are my glory." **The Bhagavad Gita**

"That one is dear to me who runs not after the pleasant or away from the painful, grieves not, lusts not, but lets things come and go as they happen." **The Bhagavad Gita**

"Actions do not cling to me because I am not attached to their results. Those who understand this and practice it live in freedom." **The Bhagavad Gita**

"Calmness, gentleness, silence, self-restraint, and purity: these are the disciplines of the mind." **The Bhagavad Gita**

"Fill your mind with me; love me; serve me; worship me always. Seeking me in your heart, you will at last be united with me." **The Bhagavad Gita**

"Anger leads to bewilderment, bewilderment to loss of memory of true Self, and by that intelligence is destroyed, and with the destruction of intelligence he perishes." **The Bhagavad Gita**

Made in the USA
Middletown, DE
28 November 2019